GREAT INDIAN LIVES

SUBHASH CHANDRA BOSE

JAICO PUBLISHING HOUSE

Ahmedabad Bangalore Chennai
Delhi Hyderabad Kolkata Mumbai

Published by Jaico Publishing House
A-2 Jash Chambers, 7-A Sir Phirozshah Mehta Road
Fort, Mumbai - 400 001
jaicopub@jaicobooks.com
www.jaicobooks.com

SUBHASH CHANDRA BOSE
ISBN 81-7224-507-6

First Jaico Impression: 2005
Third Jaico Impression: 2016

Printed by
Trinity Academy For Corporate Training Limited, Mumbai

I

Subhash Chandra Bose was born in a Bengali family on January 23rd, 1897, at Cuttack in Orissa. He spent the first sixteen years of his life there.

This was a time of terrible violence in the area.

Religious reforms were taking place. The unhappiness of being ruled by the British was spreading amongst many people. Because of all this terrorism became the order of the day.

Bengal was partitioned in 1905. The people of Bengal were enraged. They took it as an insult to the rich tradition of culture and harmony that had prevailed for centuries.

Had Bengalies no religion, no self-respect? Racial hatred began to take root. Terrorism became the final act. It was the only way out for those who were

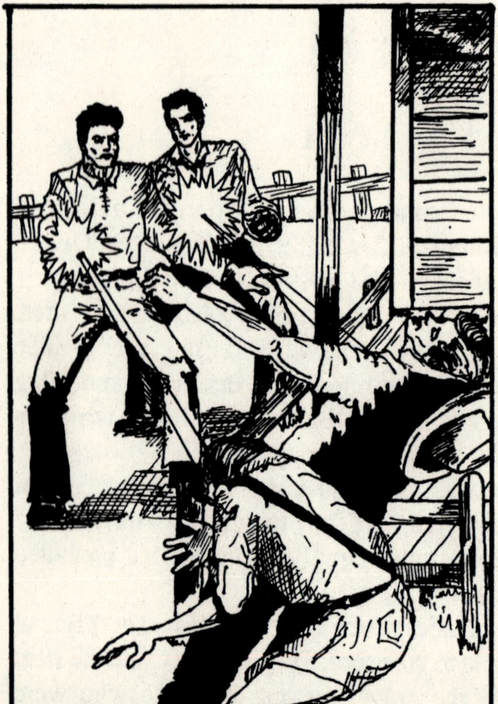

Magistrates and police officers were attacked.

enslaved, without a hope for justice.

The revolutionaries collected arms and manufactured bombs. They went to schools and colleges throughout Bengal and encouraged youngsters to join terrorist clubs. Every year the violence increased.

Money was stolen to support the terrorist organisations. Magistrates and police officers were attacked. No longer did the nationalist believe in a peaceful liberation. Military power was taken as the only hope of achieving freedom.

The Partition was replaced in 1911. Even though this cooled tempers a little, there was no peace. The target was now foreign rule.

Bengal dreamt of revolt and her poets sang great songs of freedom. These were the songs composed during Bose's boyhood, and he must have heard them often.

Subhash's father, Jankinath Bose, was an able, public-spirited lawyer, and believed in orthodox nationalism. From 1905 he became the Public Prosecutor in Cuttack, and from 1912 a member of

He was able to spend more time on gardening and nature study.

the Bengal Legislative Council. He was a man of moderate means and of great ambition for his eight sons and six daughters.

Bose's mother was a strong, sensible woman, who ruled her large family firmly. The sixth son, Subhash stood in awe of his father and mother. In a disciplined home, Subhash learnt to respect hard work and good behaviour.

Before he was five, Subhash was sent to the Baptist Missionary School which his brothers attended. Here for seven years he underwent a normal English education. He was an intelligent child. But he was not able to excel in sports and this made him sad.

But now Bengali had become a compulsory subject in order to pass the metric final exam in Calcutta. So when he was twelve years old, Subhash was sent to an Indian School, in order to prepare for this exam.

In the new school, Subhash was not left alone to brood about his failure at games. Instead he was able to spend more time on gardening and nature study, which he enjoyed very much.

He started reading all he could find of Vivekanand.

He was a quiet, serious boy, who loved to read a lot. He used to think a lot about himself and the world around him. He was fascinated with religious truth and self-control. He used to look at the sadhus and pilgrims of Puri, the holy city near his home, and wonder about Yoga, meditation and mysticism.

He was also very compassionate, and even at this young age, he would rush to do some social service. The first hints of politics and struggle for independence began, and he even made contacts with secret societies of Calcutta.

Thus at a rather tender age, he began to wonder at the difference between being a man of action and the mystic world of the sadhus. This became a little clearer when, at the age of fifteen, he came upon by chance, the writings of Swami Vivekanand, who spoke of salvation through service — service to humanity and particularly to Mother India.

He started reading all that he could find written on Vivekanand and Vivekanand's master, the saintly Ramkrishna Parmahansa. Selfless service became his

He went with a friend through northern India.

ideal. In 1913, he joined the Presidency College in Calcutta to study philosophy.

In 1914, unknown to his family, he went with a friend to northern India, looking for a spiritual master to show him his way. But the holy place of Hinduism held no leader for him. Soon after he returned to his sorrowing family thinking. "I have some mission to fulfill; but I must find it!"

He was already a leader among the students.

II

After his return from his pilgrimage; politics began to assert its hold on Subhash. He was already a leader among the students, playing a full part in college life.

He started a debating club saying, "The country will need great debators, parliamentarians — when we are free that is. "He wanted to encourage quick thinking.

He said, "We Indians are too dependent on others — for action, views, initiative, everything." And so he stressed on self-reliance — to develop a confidence in oneself.

With his friends, he was not always talkative. But during arguments, or in the debating club, his speech was warm and urgent. He was passionately eager for

An assault on one of the English lecturers.

social service, kept aloof from the secret societies, and with a certain loftiness of character, seemed to move towards a life of deep philosophic thinking and meditation.

Then there occurred the incident which Bose afterwards called the turning point of his career: he was expelled from his college for his leading part in an assault on one of the English lecturers.

The lecturer had made certain remarks that had angered the students. Hostility had grown, and there had been angry protests from the students. Bose had led these protests. The students were excited and militant — they felt that this was the supreme test of the manhood of Indian youth, and hence of India's own future.

"India has entered a new life ...," wrote Bose at this time. "Blessed are we that we are living in this auspicious hour... Cast off despair and look beyond to the new before us, and follow it."

Such a mood in a pupil really worried the college. Tension increased. Soon after, an angry lecturer dealt

He thought of all the other incidents where the English rulers had made Indians suffer.

rather roughly with a group of noisy students on the verandah outside his classroom.

That afternoon a party of students assaulted one of the friends of the lecturer. Bose had been present, and automatically was held responsible for leading the group.

Bose neither denied this nor did he apologise. And so, in February 1916, he was expelled.

The punishment was perhaps not without reason. But for Bose, it was the worst tragedy. He felt that he had been punished and insulted only because he was an Indian fighting for the dignity of his Motherland. He accepted his punishment without protest and left for Cuttack.

But the injury was not forgotten. He was nineteen years old then and racial hatred ate into his soul. He thought of all the other incidents where the English rulers had made Indians suffer and his blood boiled.

He remembered the words spoken against him by the college authorities — "the most disturbing element in the college" they had called him. "Well, that was

He joined the University Training Corps.

nothing," he thought to himself. "He would create other disturbance for them to remember!"

His sole aim now was to show himself superior to the white-faced foreigner. India also must show herself superior. To help India accomplish this was, he felt, in some way his mission.

Meanwhile academic studies of course, made little progress. His father had been sympathetic to what had happened. But he was firm that Subhash should not continue his studies elsewhere.

And so, in July 1917, Bose was readmitted to the University. After this there was no further setback. He joined the University Training Corps, spending many happy days in it during 1918. He also joined the Students' Consultative Committee and in 1919 achieved first-class honours in philosophy.

Being a good student, it was obvious that nothing could Bose lose from further studies. To his father it was also clear that the nationalist movement in Bengal would tempt his son deeply. And so he thought, "It is better that Subhash goes to England and sits

At Cambridge, Bose began to make English friends.

for the Indian Civil Service: power and dignity will cure him."

The father's decision was sudden, and Subhash was in a fix wondering what to do. He knew many terrorists and he also knew that the time was not ripe for violent revolution.

After thinking a lot, he agreed to go. The examination was in a way the final test of proving his superior intelligence to the foreigners.

In England he found further examples of racial hatred. And although this feeling reduced with time, he was never able to hold his patience with the British.

At Cambridge, Bose began to make English friends. In spite of himself he was impressed. "People here have a sense of time," he wrote. "Many are their defects, but one must bow one's head to their merits."

He admired their energy and love of discipline. He felt that Indians ought to improve their social manners, and in some way thought — we have to be civilised enough in England.

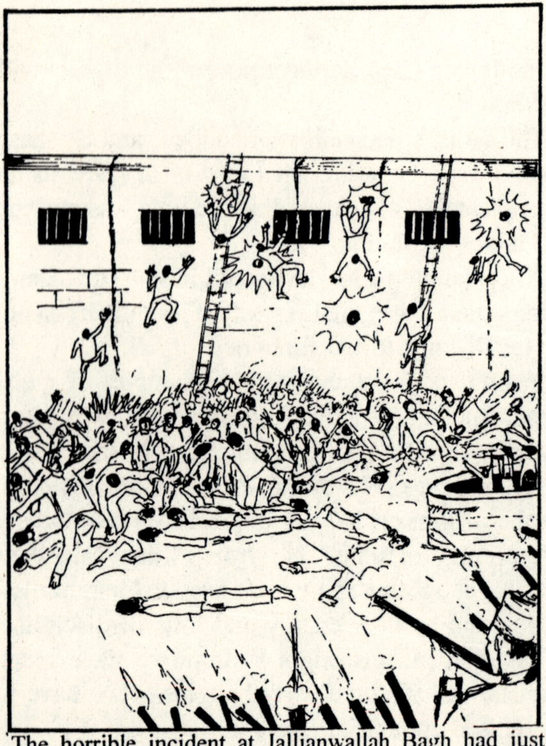

The horrible incident at Jallianwallah Bagh had just taken place at Amritsar.

III

In 1920 Bose passed the Civil Service open examination, and stood fourth, a tremendous achievement for someone who had been in England for barely eight months. But the fight for independence in India was now changing.

When Subhash had left for England, Mahatma Gandhi had not been so openly defiant of British rule. But the horrible incident at Jallianwallah Bagh had just taken place at Amritsar — hundreds of people who had gathered to join in a peaceful protest meeting, had been killed under the rampant outburst of gun firing ordered by General Dyer.

Of course official action was taken against General Dyer, who insisted that his aim had been to check the spread of rebellion amongst Indians. And a vast

Gandhiji called upon all Indians to give up their British titles and appointments.

majority of the English people as a whole appeared to support what he had done.

At this stage, Gandhiji decided that there was no hope of amicability. The Indian National Congress announced his programme of *non-cooperation*. Gandhiji also called upon all Indians to give up their British titles and appointments.

Subhash thought about this, and discussed the matter with his family, particularly with his brother Sarat. Even Sarat urged him not to resign. "Life in the Civil Service will not be bad," he said. "There is honourable work to be done," he continued. "The British mood is changing."

But Subhash replied, "I must either leave this rotten service and dedicate myself whole-heartedly to the country's cause, or I must bid good-bye to all my dreams and ideals."

No Indian had yet resigned from the Indian Civil Service. "I have no wordly ambitions at heart," he thought. "If I fail here I will never respect myself again."

The Under-Secretary of State for India sent for him.

Nothing else was worth considering. He did not intend to marry, and this was a part of his mission. His mind was made up in January 1921: he would offer himself to work at the Congress National College in Calcutta, and also for the new nationalist paper, "Swaraj".

He resigned from the Indian Civil Service in April 1921.

The Under-Secretary of State for India sent for him. Bose told him, "I do not think one can be loyal to the British raj and yet serve India honestly, heart and soul."

His father was very upset. But Subhash had seen similar scenes in the past too, and was not diverted. He said, "If we build our ideals thinking of nation first and last of our family happiness, won't the ideals be wonderful!"

He returned to India in July 1921, to throw himself at the feet of Gandhiji. Gandhiji had just announced his promise of freedom for India within a year. Bose was enthused and excited. He felt that Gandhiji wanted to start a battle.

So that when Bose returned to India, it was with all the fire and energy of a revolutionary. Eager to prove himself, he wanted to be called upon for some deed of daring that would show him and his family, his great sacrifice, of his brilliance in the Civil Service.

He found Gandhiji in Bombay, and he was so fascinated that he wrote, "I remember clearly the scene of that afternoon... Facing the door sat the Mahatma, surrounded by some of his closest followers. All were wearing home-made khadi. As I entered I felt somewhat out of place in my foreign costume. But the Mahatma received me with his typical hearty smile and soon put me at ease, and the conversation started at once. I wanted to know about his plan, which would finally lead to overthrowing foreign rule. And so I heaped question upon question and the Mahatma replied with his patience."

But instead of action, he found non-violence, instead of a plan for battle, the impossible hope that the British would change by Gandhiji's methods. Bose left him disappointed. He returned home to Calcutta to work under C.R. Das, the Bengali freedom fighter, who had given up his flourishing legal practice, to work for the country's freedom. With Das, Bose was to learn many lessons.

With Das, Bose was to learn many lessons.

IV

At this point it is important to understand the reasons for the rising discontent amongst Indians against the British. After all it was not without reason that a brilliant young man like Bose had resigned from the highest service to which he could have aspired.

And there were others — those whose fathers had worked sincerely for Indians against the British, but who for themselves found only the way of revolt.

Indian subjugation had been stated as the aim of British rule for a hundred years. A number of changes had been brought in by the British, by which Indians were included in the Government. But the overall impression seemed to be that inspite of all that was being done, the intention to leave India was not there at all.

The First World War broke out in 1914.

Meanwhile, the changes that were taking place made Indians strongly feel that they could do without the British, that they were very capable of managing on their own.

When the First World War broke out in 1914, the mood in India was one of despair. Some thought that open revolt was the only answer. Others continued to hope for a peaceful transfer. Then in August 1917, the British government decided to take some more steps towards allowing Indians to govern their own land.

Mr. Edwin Montangue, the Secretary of State for India came to hold discussions with the Viceroy. Both of them tried to bring about change which would be accepted by the British Parliament as well as the Indians.

But they were also quick to note a change in the Indian mind. "There is the bitterness of feeling that has grown because the Englishman does not think the Indian his equal," they noted. And this feeling could not be changed by reforms in the government. It would

He worked hard under the guidance of Mr.C.R.Das.

have had to come about after a long period of understanding between the two communities. And this was not to be.

Meanwhile, in 1919, the Rowlatt Bill was introduced. The strongest possible protest came from the Indians. It started a chain of events that was to change a lot of things.

Unrest in Punjab, followed by the massacre at Amritsar in 1920, convinced the Indians that they had been cheated — they would never believe Britain again.

It was in this explosive atmosphere that Subhash Chandra Bose entered Indian politics in 1921. For the next two years he worked hard under the guidance of Mr. C.R. Das in the Congress National College, of which he was Principal, on the newspaper "Swaraj", and also as a member in charge of publicity of Bengal Provincial Congress Committee.

Mr. C:R. Das was a more aggressive freedom fighter than Gandhiji — in fact the Calcutta wing of the Congress was more disturbed than that of the

Civil disobedience started in Bengal on December 1st.

Congress as a whole.

C.R. Das immediately took a liking for Bose, and in no time at all, he was totally immersed in the work of the Congress at Calcutta. He attended Gandhiji's secret conference in September 1921, taking down the Mahatma's answers, and listening to his instructions for the new non-cooperation programme.

He led the protest against the Prince of Wales' visit to India, and organised the Congress Volunteers in Calcutta. These Volunteers were soon declared illegal.

"I feel the handcuffs on my wrists," said C.R. Das, "and the weight of iron on my body. It is the agony of being a slave."

Civil disobedience — i.e. openly disobeying rules set by the British — started in Bengal on December 1st.

On December 10th, Bose was arrested for parading illegally. "Only six months," he said to the magistrate in disappointment; is it because I have stolen a chicken?"

Mr. Das was arrested at the same time and he and Bose spent most of the imprisonment together. Bose

Bose spent six weeks working day and night in the flooded regions of Northern Bengal.

served his leader even in jail — cooking his food, and learning how to bear discomfort and hardship. Das showed a sympathy and patience for others that impressed Bose greatly. For Bose, he came to take the place of the 'guru' he had been in search for such a long time.

They talked a lot about the freedom struggle, and also about what they would do once they were released from jail. They were extremely upset when Gandhiji called for a halt in the civil disobedience movement. Once both Bose and Das were released, they started asking the Congress to follow this course.

In September 1922, Bose spent six weeks working day and night in the flooded regions of Northern Bengal. His unflaging energy in the presence of suffering and his ability to organise work won him lasting gratitude. He was soon famous in his region for his selfless service.

Das resigned and formed his own party-the Swaraj ya Party

V

At the Congress Assembly of December 1922, C.R. Das was the President. He put forth his idea of winning election and then seeing how to destroy the British from within. Bose was his secretary and actively supported him.

But although Gandhiji was in jail, his influence against 'council entry' as it was called, was too strong. A month later Das resigned and formed his own party — the Swarajya Party or the Self-government Party. They decided to fight the elections in 1923.

The Swarajya Party was still part of the Congress, and because of the name perhaps, the party was very successful in the elections. At the beginning of 1924, it even formed a small but strong group in the Central Legislature in Delhi.

Meanwhile in April 1924, the Swarajists won control of the Calcutta Corporation. Das became Mayor of Calcutta and Subhash was elected as the Chief Executive Officer. Under its new constitution, the Corporation of Calcutta was in a position to decide a lot of things on its own.

Bose found himself in an important post with wide powers and a salary of 3,000 British Pound Sterling. At the age of twenty-seven he was thus in a far more important position than any which he would have got in the Indian Civil Service for many years.

The new Indian administrators wore Congress home-spun khadi, reduced their own salaries, renamed streets and public places after Indian heroes, improved the educations, social welfare and public health services.

But his downfall was being plotted. In 1923, violence erupted in Bengal once again. The Swarjists were believed to be actively involved in terrorism. In 1924, the situation grew worse, and the police could do little.

The old days of terror returned.

He would receive different visitors even late at night.

The old days of terror returned. In March 1924 Gopinath Saha was executed for terrorists murder. There was no doubt about his guilt, but the proud way in which he accepted his sentence made a deep impression.

Taking leave of his mother, Saha said, "I beg you to pray to God, that mothers in India should give birth to sons like me, and let every home to blessed by a mother like you."

Nearing the gallows, he said, "May every drop of my blood sow the seeds of freedom in every home in India."

Although Bose officially proclaimed that terrorism was not right, he would not help being moved by Saha's words. In his office Bose met all kinds of people. He knew many of the revolutionaries; he would receive different visitors even late at night.

Soon the British started suspecting him of having links with the terrorists. Bose had never been actively involved with terrorist activities. But when in October 1924, the suspected terrorist leaders were rounded

"I felt one had not only to be lenient to one's enemies, but also to love them."

up, Bose was arrested as one of the most dangerous.

There were strong protests against his arrest. For two months, Bose served in the Alipore Jail. Then, in January 1925, he was removed with seven others to the great fort of Mandalay in Burma.

But it was not easy. For quite some time, he felt the injustice of his imprisonment. Then he turned towards studying his motive and actions.

He wrote, "The change in me was this, that I decided to be honest. I decided to watch my own movements. And I learnt that even in the thick of fight (since fight one must) one had not only to be lenient to one's enemies, but also to love them."

With this realisation came a new moral strength. In June 1925, he was deeply struck by the sudden death of C. R.. Das. "I gave him my heart's deep devotion and reverent love not so much because I happened to be his follower in Politics, as because I happened to know him in his private life," he wrote.

This was a terrible loss for the Youth of Bengal. It was as deep a loss for Bose as well, who had never

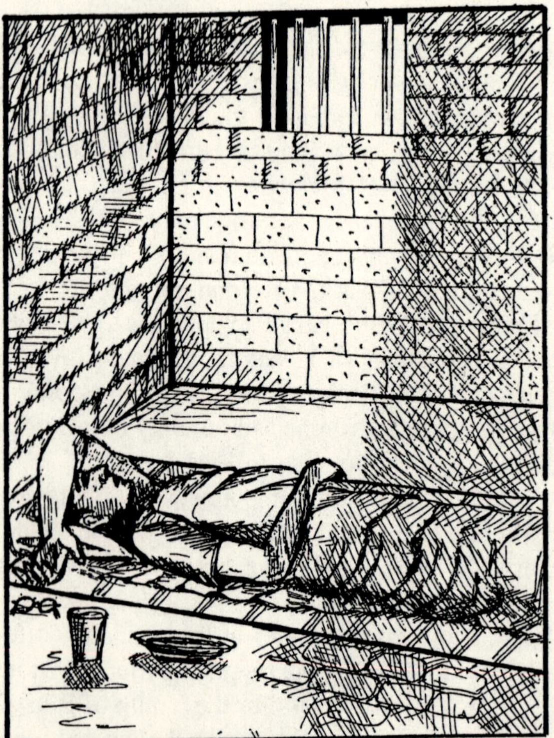

Already his health was failing.

been on his own till then.

At the end of 1926, he was nominated as a candidate for the Bengal Legislative Assembly: his friends hoped that his election would force the government to release him. But this move failed.

The great red-brick fort of Mandalay, with its fairy-tale royal palace which he could see from his room, was to hold Bose for a few months more. Already his health was failing. In 1927 it broke down, and the Government of Bengal offered to release him, provided he would go to Switzerland without setting foot in India.

This he refused with contempt. In a letter to his brother he wrote, "I am not a shopkeeper and I do not bargain... I do not attach such importance to my health, that I should try to save it by haggling over it... Our Cause is of freedom and truth. Our bodies many fail and perish, but with faith undiminished and will unconquerable, triumph will be ours."

He was in any case too ill to go to Switzerland without recovering fully. It was because of this that he was set free on May 16th.

By November he was fit enough to be drawn into full political activity, and was elected Chairman of the Bengal Provincial Congress Committee.

VI

The two years spent in Mandalay were among the most important years in his life. He had come there with very little political maturity, still looking to his guru for guidance.

When he left prison in 1927, he had a clear political understanding of his own. Mr. Das was dead and Bose himself was now regarded as the natural leader of Bengal. From the first he had realised that his imprisonment would not be all loss.

He returned bursting with confidence, strength, and eloquence. "There is no power on earth which can keep India in bondage any longer," her shouted; "Sacrifice your life at the altar of freedom; India shall be free, the only question is when."

Bose knew the importance of his audience. He never doubted the authority of the crowd, if they agreed with what he was saying. Because of this, he

"There is no power on earth which can keep India in bondage any longer."

could carry a crowd with him, and then himself be carried away by the enthusiasm he had generated.

1928 had given Bose new opportunities for working in the Congress. With Jawaharlal Nehru, he had become a General Secretary of the Congress in December 1927.

He addressed the youth of the country, and painted for them his own picture of freedom. His speeches were fiery and skilful. His stature as a leader was more widely accepted. He commanded the parade of 'Congress Volunteers' at the 1928 Congress Assembly. The smartness and precision of the marching volunteers impressed even the peace-loving Congressmen.

He still kept away from women except to enrol them in the political struggle. It was said that he had decided not to marry till India achieved independence. This and his refusal to touch alcohol became a definite part of his public reputation.

In October 1929, the Viceroy, Lord Irwin stated that India would attended the Round Table Conference in England in the process of the British Dominion.

He commanded the parade of 'Congress Volunteers'.

But this did not come through. And in 1930 fullscale civil disobedience started.

Bose was arrested on his birthday, January 23rd, for leading an 'Independence' procession, and sentenced to a year's imprisonment. In jail he once again mixed quietly with his Congress friends, reading, meditating, writing, praying in a scheduled corner of the prison room.

There were incidents even in prison. He was injured in April when he took the side of some prisoners who were being roughly handled by the jail staff; in July he staged a hunger strike against prison treatment. But apart from this he managed to rest — as rest he badly needed.

When he emerged from prison on September 25th, he was Mayor of Calcutta, because the man who had been elected Mayor before, could not take the oath within six months. For the next three months he was busy with his work as Mayor and also the welfare of civil disobedience prisoners.

Early 1931, he was arrested for visiting disturbed

He was injured and arrested while leading a demonstration on 26th January.

area of Bengal, which had been forbidden to him. He had hardly been released when he was injured and arrested while leading a demonstration on 26th January — which had been declared as 'Independence Day'.

A senior police officer has warned him not to take part. He sent a message back to the police officer through the messenger — "Tell your boss," he said, "that I will break the law."

In court the next day, he spoke strongly about the bad conditions in the prison room in which he had spent the night. He could not have done so as a Congressman, but he could as Mayor.

Six weeks later he was released with other political prisoners under the Gandhi-Irwin Pact-an agreement between Gandhiji and Lord Irwin, the Viceroy of India.

All was peaceful for ten months after this. Then, in December 1931, Gandhiji returned to India after the Second Round Table Conference, and there led to a new trial of strength.

While Gandhiji was busy with discussion at the

He wrote to a friend, "The price of freedom is suffering and sacrifice."

Conference, Bose had kept quiet. But as the unrest of 1931 began to grow, he started troubling the government in Bengal. He disobeyed British orders openly, ignored the officers who tried to stop him, and was able to track down injustice, cruelty and oppression, whereever it was happening.

He was naturally arrested, along with other Congressmen, on January 2nd, 1932. Two days earlier he had written to a friend:

"Do you want the beautiful scent of a rose in full bloom? If so, you must accept the thorns.

Do you want to see the bounty of the smiling dawn? If so, you must live through the dark hours of the night.

Do you want the joy of freedom? If so, you must pay the price. And the price of freedom is suffering and sacrifice."

None was readier than Subhash Chandra Bose to pay that price. He had never spared a thought for himself. The years after his release from Mandalay had taken every bit that he could offer.

He went to Europe for his medical treatment.

VII

By the end of 1932, he was again gravely ill; on February 22nd he was released, on the condition that he went to Europe for his medical treatment. This time he agreed and entered Dr. Furth's hospital in Vienna on March 11th.

The doctors felt that his condition was serious, and prescribed a long course of treatment. At this time, Subhash met Mr. Vithaldas Patel, a great Congressman and patriot, who was also there in Vienna for treatment.

The two men kept a close watch on events in India. In April, Gandhiji undertook a fast to force certain of his views on his countrymen. He was also released for reasons of health. On May 8th, he stopped the civil disobedience movement for which he had gone to prison in 1932.

"No real change in history has ever been achieved by discussions."

To Bose and Patel in Vienna, this was a cowardly surrender. They drafted a joint statement, which declared Gandhiji as a failure. Bose felt that the Round Table Conference had been a waste of time, for said he, "no real change in history has ever been achieved by discussions." — "But the only alternative is war!" — "What is it? India can well afford to bring a blood sacrifice for her freedom. 350 million miserable lives are waiting to be set free."

"There speaks the minds of young India," said Patel, "it may be a brilliant mind and it may be foolish one. It may be creative and it may be suicidal. But it is here, and if the Gods are thirsty what can we do but offer our blood?"

It was time for a new deal in the Congress and a new leader. Neither Bose nor Patel hoped for much immediate progress in India. Both thought that the best chance was in letting people abroad know what was happening in India. They hoped that world opinion might force the British to relax their grip.

Bose would have liked to go further than this, and

He visited Berlin, Rome, Prague, Warsaw, Istanbul, Belgrade and Bucharest.

was very tempted to accept an offer put forth by the Russians. Not that Bose was a communist, but was willing to learn all that Russia could teach him of revolutionary technique, and to accept any help she could offer against the British.

Patel stopped him for he saw clearly that such a link would hinder Bose's service to India.

But there were others who could be asked for help. In May, Bose obtained permission to go to Germany. He visited Berlin, Rome, Prague, Warsaw, Istanbul, Belgrade and Bucharest. In the next two years he even visited some of these countries for a second time.

Meanwhile, in October, 1933, Mr. Vithalbhai Patel died, and he left for Bose not only some of his ideas, but also a lot of money for spreading the knowledge of India abroad. Bose was very touched by his friend's confidence and worked harder to make his foreign contacts.

He called impatiently on his friend, Dilip Kumar Roy, to leave his yogic meditation, and help him in the work of trying to spread India's message abroad.

"We hope to make peace with Britain." they said.

Gone was the calmness of mind. He was sure his way was right—nothing else mattered, nobody else knows better.

He wrote without stopping, of India's rights, asking people to help in the fight against injustices. He could not bear to see suffering. He took a lot of interest in the Indians in Europe, urging the students especially never to forget that they were India's ambassadors abroad.

He organised Students' Association which was to help Indians allover the continent. Those in Berlin who had suffered because of the Nazis, never forgot his help and inspiration.

Wherever he could, Bose made political contacts. He met noted persons like Dr. Benes and Mr. De Valera. He visited and was much encouraged by M. Romain Rolland. He was received by Adolf Hitler, Ribbentrop, and others in the Nazi ruling party.

He asked the Nazis when they were going to attack Britain, "so that," said he, "we might also take up arms at the same time against the British." The

Gandhiji had turned from active politics to village welfare.

Germans said they had not thought of this. "We hope to make peace with Britain," they said.

In the end Bose told them: "Britain is our enemy. We will fight her whether you support us or not." He had no doubt that war would come to Europe.

Meanwhile, Gandhiji had turned from active politics to village welfare. Some of the Congress leaders followed him, some remained in jail, some thought once more of working for freedom by peaceful means.

The more radical freedom fighters, the men who would have followed Bose if he had been in India formed the Congress Socialist Party in 1934. Bose however felt that no reform, no new party within the Congress would now serve. He no longer believed that fighting elections and gaining power in the government would achieve anything.

"In India we want a party that will not only work for India's freedom, but also produce a national constitution, and after winning freedom will put into operation the whole programme of national rebuilding," said Bose.

At the end of 1934, Bose flew to India.

VIII

In November 1934, Bose published his own account of Indian nationalism in a book called "The Indian Struggle'. In this he pointed a new way for India. Bose had been stirred by what he had seen in Rome and Istanbul — a strong party organisation in Rome and Mustapha Kemal's swift modernisation of a backward country in Istanbul.

He felt that at this time India required a dictator. He said, "There must be a strong Central Government with dictatorial powers for some years to come.

Government by a strong party bound together while she was achieving freedom!

At the end of 1934, Bose flew to India because his father was seriously unwell. But he could not meet his father, who died a little before Bose could reach

He set sail for Europe on January 10th 1935.

his bedside.

Ria Bhadur Jankinath Bose had long ago accepted his brilliant son and had learnt to be proud of the noted rebel he had become. Subhash would have had to remain in India for a longer time. But he would have had to go back to prison, and he set sail for Europe on January 10th 1935.

During this year, his health improved a lot and by the end of the year, the desire to re-enter the freedom struggle in India was difficult to resist. He made up his mind at the beginning of 1936.

Jawaharlal Nehru who was the President of the Congress, urged him to come back. Congress was to discuss whether to take part in the new elections. Subhash felt that he had to come back to make sure that Congress did not take a soft stand with the British.

In March 1936 he announced that he was returning to India, and he was formally warned that he would be arrested as soon as he landed in the country. He did not care.

On April 8th, he reached Bombay and was arrested.

After his release he went to the hills and stayed there until October.

He was shouting to the crowds who waited for him: "Keep the flag of India's freedom flying."

No amount of protest resulted in his release for the British government said, "Mr. Bose is a man who, while of great ability, has always directed his ability to destructive purposes."

He was released on March 17th, 1937. There was a change in him: he had learnt the importance of talking to simple people and to value them. The term in prison had made Subhash milder.

The Congress had just emerged victorious from the first elections under the Act of 1935. Bose took little part in all the moves that followed, after Congress won the elections. After his release he went to the hills and stayed there until October, with his old friends Dr. and Mrs. Dharamvir.

Gandhiji asked him to accept the nomination as Congress President in 1938. In January 1938, he visited England. In London he was welcomed by Mr. Attlee, Mr. Ernest Bevin and Sir Stafford Cripps. A reception was held to honour him at Dorchester.

The rift with Gandhi was bound to come.

Bose was now held in high esteem. After Gandhiji and Jawaharlal Nehru, he was the next Indian politician whom the world recognised. Within India he appealed to some more than Gandhi and Nehru.

At the early age of 41, being nominated as President of the Congress by Gandhiji was in itself an achievement. It also showed that Mahatma Gandhi realised that he would have to consolidate the Congres by including the followers of Bose in Bengal and elsewhere.

Bose realised his strength. He knew that as President of Congress he would have to protect the unity of the party. But he also meant to change some of its policies.

Obviously, the rift with Gandhi was bound to come. This was the second turning point in his life.

He was disappointed that Gandhiji gave him no order for 'action'.

IX

Bose had always set himself up as an enemy of the British Raj. But as time went on he also got distanced from Gandhiji's ideas. He felt that the Congress needed an energetic leadership.

It had all started in 1921, during Bose's first meeting with Gandhi, on returning from Cambridge. He was disappointed that Gandhiji gave him no orders for 'action' — here he was, eager to do anything for the country, after sacrificing a comfortable career — and Gandhiji had said there was nothing to be done.

Not all Gandhi's followers felt that anything would be achieved by sitting quietly. But they hoped that once civil disobedience started, they could convert it into something more active. Bose was one of them.

But when Gandhiji withdrew his programme, Bose

"Only our cooperation enables a handful of Englishmen to rule our country."

was terribly upset. While in Mandalay he felt that Gandhiji's political career was bound soon, with his imprisonment in 1922. Non-violence did not appeal to Bose. He felt that British would never give in unless confronted with force.

In 1928, when both Gandhiji and Bose were back from prison, Bose spoke to Gandhi about his plan of action. "Only our cooperation enables a handful of Englishmen to rule our country," he told Gandhiji who did not agree.

With time Bose was taking more directly against Gandhiji. "Holy men would always hold an honoured place in India," he said, "but it is not their lead we shall have to follow if we are to create a new India at once — free, happy and great... We have to live in the present.

He politely opposed the Dominion Status question — of India being a part of British Dominion. He felt that this was not complete freedom. But this explanation was not accepted.

During 1929, when he spoke of his own ideas of

Let the Congress be made into a second Government.

what the freedom struggle was to be, the Congress felt that Bose was being defiant. In October 1929, he refused to sign the All Parties reply to the Viceroy's plan on Dominion Status.

With this he lost important supporter, Jawaharlal Nehru. Nehru had signed after Gandhi had managed to convince him.

When the Assembly met, Gandhiji declared that complete independence was the Congress goal. "But," said Bose, "the programme laid down by Gandhiji is not such as to carry us towards the goal of complete independence."

He put forward his own ideas — Let the Congress be made into a second Government just like the Central Government which was under the British. For this the party would have to be expanded, the people in support would have to be organised. Then, civil disobedience would totally halt normal working of the government. The Congress would be the only party capable of controlling the country, and the British would have to leave.

Bose traveled with Gandhi.

But all these ideas were rejected. Many who would have sided with Bose otherwise, went to Gandhiji who now rejected the Dominion Status. No one even realised that Bose had been rejecting Dominion Status all along.

Bose was supported only by 62 members, and he walked out with them in protest: only 62, but Gandhi could sense the strong feeling they had. With the support of so many behind him, Gandhiji could afford to let Bose go.

But realising that it was only a matter of time that others felt similar to Bose and his followers, Gandhiji started the civil disobedience campaign in 1930. Bose felt there was some hope.

Bose was aware of Gandhi's popularity. After the Gandhi-Irwin Pact, Bose traveled with Gandhi and wrote: "I wonder if such a welcome was ever given to a leader anywhere else. He stood out before the people not merely as a Mahatma but as the hero of a political fight."

In the autumn of 1931, the British people saw

Civil disobedience was re-started.

Gandhi's scanty clad figure and perhaps for the first time realised that they had to do something seriously about India's problem. As such the Round Table Conference was unsuccessful. 1931 was a troubled year of India — there was unrest and the government tried to clamp down on everything. Gandhiji, back from London on December 28th, complained about this. It was against everything signed for in the Gandhi — Irwin Pact.

Civil disobedience was re-started. Bose went to prison with the rest, and for fifteen months he was silent.

In April 1933, Bose along with Vithalbhai Patel in Vienna had protested against Gandhiji's methods. This was the strongest opposition to Gandhi that any Congressman had dared to utter.

Bose felt that Gandhiji had failed, because of a number of reasons. He had not understood his enemies; he had not made a plan; he had not asked for help abroad.

There were others like Bose who felt that Gandhi

would not control the Congress after 1933. But at this stage, even though Gandhi was no longer leader of the Congress party, he was still important so as to decide the thinking in the party, especially through Jawaharlal Nehru.

But even Nehru could not use the Mahatma's words so easily — after all till as late as 1929 he was as opposed to Gandhi's thinking as Bose was.

X

Around this time, Sardar Patel's strong guidance took the Congress to the social and administrative life of the country. Bose had long ago urged that it should be so.

In the elections of 1936, the Congress gained a majority in seven out of the eleven provinces and emerged as the strongest party. Gandhiji returned to active politics in March 1937.

This was the same time Bose returned to the Indian political scene — after his recover yin Vienna and further imprisonment in India.

Gandhiji knew that Bose was the only national figure capable of dividing the Congress. And this was still possible. Bose could no longer be ignored. The two met in Calcutta for a long discussion.

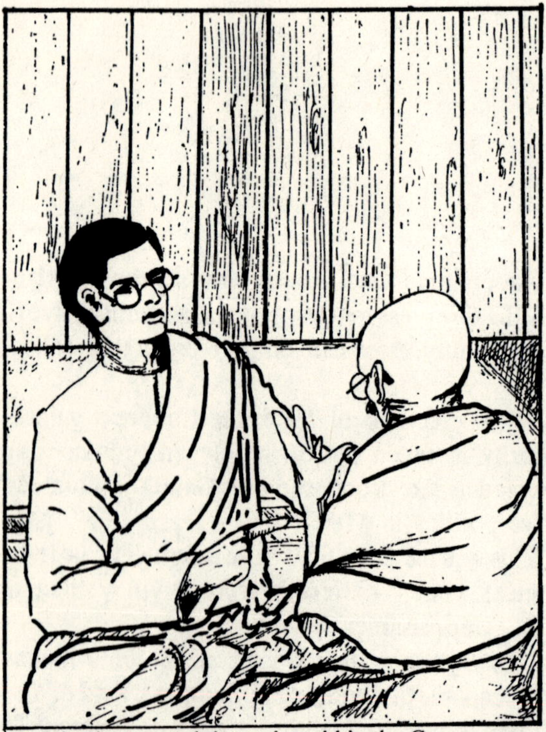

Both leaders agreed that unity within the Congress was important.

Bose accepted Gandhi's proposal to be President of the Congress. Both leaders agreed that unity within the Congress was important. Bose knew that to oppose the British it was important to fight together. He agreed with Gandhiji that the Federation of India which had been suggested would leave the real control to the British — so this would have to be rejected. Bose also now accepted that the framing of the Indian constitution should be left to an Indian Constituent Assembly, after the British had left.

In 1938, Bose was made the President of the 51st Congress at Haripura. This was a proud and touching moment for Bose. Those who cheered for the new President saw him tough, his burning enthusiasm, his humanity. Bose also felt in his heart his new relationship with Gandhi.

In his speech, he did not say anything about a new party or about reforming the old one. Gandhiji was still referred as the Mahatma who would lead the country to independence.

But he also spoke of the importance of keeping

Bose was made the President of the 51st Congress at Haripura.

hold on power won at independence. He was keen that a plan be made for rebuilding the country after independence. Gandhi was not too happy about this, but Jawaharlal Nehru supported it.

About Britain, Bose said what Gandhi himself felt: "We have no enmity towards the British people. We are fighting Great Britain, and we want the fullest freedom to decide our future relations with her."

But the Gandhi-Bose peace was uncertain. As 1938 wore on, the strain increased. In 1939 when stood for a re-election as Congress President, Gandhiji was unprepared. Their differences by now, were openly known. At the election, Bose's electrifying speech made him defeat Gandhi's candidate by a narrow margin.

But even as Bose entered his second year in office, Gandhi announced that the election was a personal defeat, and hinted that he no longer wanted to continue in the party.

Bose insisted that he had not wanted to oppose the Mahatma. But the working Committee decided

Bose's health crumbled yet again.

to resign and by the end of February, the work in the party was beginning to suffer.

Bose's health crumbled yet again.

When the Congress Assembly met on March 10th, Gandhi was absent and Bose was very unwell, lying on a stretcher. He could not even travel in the Presidential procession. His speech was short, without the usual energy — and had to be read out by some one else.

Some of the most important session he could not attend at all. His bold suggestion, demanding freedom for India within six months, by threatening civil disobedience, only made the Congressmen nervous. Nobody agreed and Bose was forced to seek Gandhi's approval for whatever programme he suggested.

There followed long and fruitless letters between Gandhi and Bose. Bose was unwilling to change his policy. And Gandhi was absolutely against civil disobedience at this stage — to him violence seemed in the air, and he would not knowingly unleash it. Bose had been open about their differences. Gandhiji

His speech had to be read out by some one else.

was even more so: "How can we find any thing common on the political platform? Let us agree to differ there and meet on the social and moral platforms."

Gandhiji knew that even on the economic front, Bose had his own ideas. So he told Bose. "You need not worry; put forward your policy and name your Cabinet. You can present both to the Congress for approval.

Bose had no way but to resign.

XI

Bose knew that if the Congress was asked to choose between him and Gandhi, there could be only one result. He again begged for Gandhi's support: "If we part ways a terrible fight within will start. The Congress will become weak and the British would take advantage."

But Gandhiji was insistent that they should part. Bose had no way but to resign when he faced the All India Congress Committee at the end of April. This was a turning point in Bose's life — the second one.

The first one he claimed had been the result of British injustice. Now he felt the injustice and betrayal of his own people. After all he had been elected as President in a democratic manner — the Congress had selected him in preference to Gandhi's candidate.

He formed a new party called the 'Forward Bloc'.

Those who had voted for him had known his views and still elected him. But now, his own friends and supporters had left him—as the leader of the Congress he had been forced to accept failure. That was injustice.

Perhaps in truth he had failed — failed because with his brilliance and confidence he would have never accepted ideas which he did not believe in. "I am an extremist," he had once said, " all or nothing..."

This had always been his way: it was his strength and his weakness, and perhaps his downfall now was because of this.

But all Bose could see was the injustice. In despair he formed a new party called the 'Forward Bloc' in the Congress Party, now that the one chance of achieving independence which had come in his eighteen years of service had been rejected.

The 'Forward Bloc' was organised on Bose's own militaristic lines: it proclaimed his revolutionary ideas; it brought together much of the extremist enthusiasm of Bengal Bose had hoped that his new party would prove a strong challenge to the Congress But this was

Bose's speeches became more violent.

not so. In fact even in Bengal, Gandhiji was able to overrule him.

But now Bose openly spoke against the Congress and said that the Congress was a dictatorship not very different from Hitler's. In July he called for a country-wide demonstration against a particular Congress move. So open a challenge could hardly be ignored, and Bose was suspended from the Congress office for three years.

The Congress invited him to take part in forming a war policy. But even here, Bose put forward only his ideas, unwilling to listen to the rest. When his plans were not approved, he just walked out.

While the Congress was meeting in Ramgarh in March 1940, Bose attended another Conference held in opposition. This conference called for an immediate all-India struggle with "no rest or break."

Bose's speeches became more violent. He felt that the British no longer took the Congress seriously, because it talked, but did not act.

"With every blow that she receives in Europe, the

"Release me or I shall refuse to live."

might of Britain is bound to loosen its grip on India... Let us therefore stop talking of saving Britain with India's help. India must, in this serous time, think of herself first... It is for the Indian people to make an immediate demand for transfer of power to them."

Once the war started, Bose could no longer be left free. He was arrested on July 2nd, 1940.

Bose felt that Britain was tottering. If only India could have some military support from outside, British power could be easily crushed. But from where was this help to come?

Perhaps Russia, who very recently had suffered her own revolution might understand India's need. But for that a messenger was needed, somebody well-known, who would be taken seriously. At last he decided that he was the only one who could do this.

But first he had to get out of prison! He knew that the government would not let him die in jail. So he made a plan — he decided to starve himself to death. "Release me," he said, or I shall refuse to live — and it is for me to decide whether I choose to live or to

He had grown a neat beard.

die."

His appeal was full of feeling: "To my countrymen I say — 'Forget not that the greatest curse for a man is to remain a slave. Forget not that the biggest crime is to accept injustice and wrong. Remember that you must give life if you want to get it. And remember that the highest quality is to battle against injustice, no matter what the cost may be."

After six days of his fast, during which he drank only water with salt, Bose was allowed to go home. For a time he recovered quietly, not going out.

After some days he stopped receiving visitors. A few of his friends saw him on January 16th, and noticed that he had grown a neat beard. On January 26th, 1941, the day fixed for his trial, he was not to be found.

He was disguised as a Muslim religious teacher, the Maulvi Ziauddin,

XII

In the early hour of January 17th 1941, a car had drawn up near Bose's home in Calcutta. Quietly, while everyone was still asleep, Bose slipped out of the house. He was disguised as a Muslim religious teacher, the Maulvi Ziauddin. His small bag was loaded on to the car, and he moved away unnoticed; with him was his nephew, Sisir Kumar Bose.

And so began his escape from India.

There was no chance of going by train — for the stations were watched. He went, therefore by road, moving at night, hiding by day, to a place called Gomoh, 210 miles from Calcutta. Here he said goodbye to Sisir Kumar, and took a train to Peshawar. At Peshawar, a man called Bhagat Ram met him, and after two days took him to Kabul.

They went to Kabul disguised as Pathans.

On the way to Kabul, Bhagat Ram was dressed as a Pathan, and called himself Rehmat Khan. Bose, also in Pathan disguise, pretended to be deaf and dumb, since he could not speak the local language.

They left Peshawar in a car, and turned off the main Kabul road before Jamrud, the great fort which guards the entrance to the Khyber Pass. They took the car till the road was good. But after that they had to walk to the Afghan frontier, led by two armed Pathans.

They passed through tribal areas and spent the second night in a mosque at Adda Sharif. From here they went on a Lalpura. On the fourth day they re-crossed the Kabul River and reached the main road again, far inside Afghanistan.

By now their guides had to leave and Bose who was tired, slept on the roadside. Bhagat Ram tried all day to see if they could find a car to take them further. At last towards evening they climbed on to an open lorry, which drove through the night and all the following day, up the snowy valley to Kabul.

They took shelter in a lorry drivers inn

Half-frozen, they climbed down near the Lahore Gate, and took shelter in a lorry-drivers' inn. It was an uncomfortable night.

For the next three days they tried to reach the Russian Embassy. This was not easy. In Kabul they had no friends, nor was Bhagat Ram familiar with the local language. Most people spoke Persian and Bhagat Ram knew only Pushto. Also there was the fear, that Bose's absence in India would be noticed, and then the danger would be even greater.

The embassies were guarded. They tried to stop the Russian envoy in the street when he was driving down—but they could not explain everything properly.

The bad living conditions, his own dumb disguise, the filthy inadequate clothing, the city weather — all began to have their effect on Bose. There could be no going back — returning to India like this would only mean defeat. But he had to leave this unfriendly country somehow.

On the fifth day, Bose sent Bhagat Ram to the Italian Embassy. And here there were welcoming

They asked an Indian, Mr.Uttam Chand for help.

smiles, congratulations and promises of a passport.

Bose's disappearance became known in Calcutta on January 26th 1941. At about the same time in Kabul, an Afghan police agent began to ask questions — about the two men who had been staying for such a long time at the lorry-driver's inn. Day after day he returned, asking for more and more bribes for keeping his mouth shut.

On February 3rd, the fear of being detected made them ask an Indian, Mr. Uttam Chand for help. Uttam Chand recognised them, but decided to take them in.

Six weeks passed and the journey was resumed. The Russians still paid no attention. The Italians seemed to be delaying. But at long last on March 18th, he got his false passport in the name of Orlando Massota and with guides sent from Europe to fetch him, Bose set out for the Russian border.

Bose went through the difficult journey without a stop, took the train to Moscow, and on March 28th, 1941, flew to Berlin. Now there was no question of asking for help from the Russians.

Hitler too had been thinking about India.

Bose was sure of a warm welcome from the Germans. By the time he reached Germany in March 1941, Hitler too had been thinking about India. He had already decided to invade Russia in June, and his Army had decided to rescue the Italians in Libya.

India was important because her men were fighting all over the Middle-East, and her importance as a military base was growing.

Ribbentrop received Bose well.

XIII

Ribbentrop received Bose well and was glad to hear of the rising tide of revolution in India.

Bose first said that he wanted to talk about anti-British ideas on the radio to be broadcast to India with a secret radio link. He wanted this to be part of the news.

He also wanted to raise his own army with Indian prisoners of war. But the Germans while wanting to help, were not keen to openly declare this friendship with India.

And without this Bose could not speak on the radio. So he decided to implement his other plan with the prisoners of war. In May, selected prisoners were brought to Berlin.

Their response was so good that Bose asked for

When Bose visited the camp in December, the troops were not friendly.

all Indian prisoners in North Africa to be brought to Germany at once. This was done. Annaburg Camp near Dresden was the place for all Indian prisoners.

When the Germans declared war against Russia, things changed. India was a powerful friend for the Germans, against Russia. The plan was that while the Germans attacked beyond Stalingrad into Central Asia to reach Uzbekistan and Afghanistan; the Indian Company would then leap ahead of the German Army and destroy the British-Indian positions in North-West India. The effect of the Indian Company supported by the Germans would lead to a collapse of the Army in India. They were sure to join forces against their old masters — turning into the ever-growing army of Free India.

In September, the Indian soldiers brought to Annaburg had to be convinced about all this. It took time. When Bose visited the camp in December, the troops were not friendly.

His speech was hardly heard. But while talking directly to the men, he found some of them eager,

It was at these gatherings that his greeting 'Jai Hind' was first used.

some who even paid homage to him, as an important Indian leader.

By January 1942, Bose had gathered round him some 25 Indian assistants. As these men arrived he had set up an office which he called the 'Indian Independence League' or 'Free India Centre'.

Here he set his men to work. Some planned radio programmes which opened as the 'secret' station, 'Azad Hind Radio' in December 1941. Others planned the study of the problems which would be faced by Free India.

Bose was a good master. He was generous and sympathetic and totally dedicated to his purpose. He saw nothing else but the ways in which to achieve his aim.

At first, Bose was hardly known in Berlin. He was still referred to as Signor Orlando Massota or His Excellency Massota. But from the beginning of 1942, he came to be known to more and more people.

There were parties and functions where the Indian community hailed him as their leader. It was at these

Meanwhile in the Far East the Japanese army had been advancing.

gatherings that his greeting 'Jai Hind' was first used.

Some of the young men wanted to join his army. Bose spoke to them of his pride in making his dream come true — of any army of free India. To all of them he was now 'Netaji', or respected leader, a title which struck to him throughout.

Meanwhile in the Far East the Japanese army had been advancing—Singapore, Rangoon, Calcutta. He felt that this was more important than the German victories in Russia and North Africa.

When Singapore fell, he made his finest broadcast from the 'secret' station — "I have waited silently and patiently; now that the hour has struck I can come forward and speak."

Bose was elated. Surely this was proof of the collapse of the British Empire: India must rejoice!

In his second 'Proclamation to the Indian People' on March 13th, Bose attacked the Mission to India led by Sir Stafford Cripps. It was an insult to India. India was for Indians — the British must quit.

A similar attack on the Cripps Mission was led

Japanese invited Bose to form a team with them.

by Rash Behari Basu from Tokyo Radio. Both men thought the Mission had failed because of their talks on the radio.

Immediately the Japanese invited Bose to form a team with them. Here was a solid support indeed. Bose met Hitler and Mussolini to discuss this. Their reply was negative. Bose urged them that India was on the brink of a revolt. He told them that he would rouse the country with his talks on radio. But Hitler felt that the time was not ripe — the distance from India was immense and the number of soldiers few. Bose realised that he would have to do some thinking. Had he after all made a mistake in leaving India? Even after setting up Free India Centres in Rome and Paris, even if he raised his army to its full strength, this achievement would be nothing in front of a German victory. Here in Berlin, he was also spied upon and his movements were suspected.

In August 1942, the Congress declared the 'Quit India Movement'.

XIV

Bose now accepted the leadership of Indians in the Far East: under the Japanese he would have control over 3 million Indians. But it took another year for him to reach the East. There was still a lot to do in Europe.

Bose made speeches on Radio which were heard in India. In these he warned the Indian soldiers and police that unless they came on the side of the freedom fighters, they would one day have to answer to the Government of Free India, for their criminal support to the British.

In August 1942, the Congress declared the 'Quit India Movement', and Bose felt that Gandhiji was now giving his blessing for the revolution.

Meanwhile the troops from of the Azad Hind Fauj

The troops from the Azad Hind Fauj were being trained.

"(Free India Army) were being trained from the Indian prisoners of war, and the numbers were growing. There were special mountain scaling and parachute jumping courses, and the older soldiers were taught how to use wireless bombs, secret inks and spying.

The main problem for the growing army was pay. At first Bose used to pay them from the money he received from the Foreign office. But now that was not enough. By September 1942, Bose had to reach an agreement with the Germans — Germany would pay the soldiers but they had to take an oath of loyalty to Hitler.

The Japanese Military Attache, Colonel Yamamote came with Bose for the First oath-taking parade. Five hundred soldiers were assembled. Each soldier had to touch his officer's sword while taking the oath.

Bose presented the Indian tri-colour flag to the soldiers — the green, white and saffron flag of the Indian National Congress; but with the figure of a springing tiger in place of the Congress spinning wheel.

"Your names will be written in golden letters in the history of Free India."

"Your names," he said, "will be written in golden letters in the history of Free India: every martyr in this holy war will have a monument there."

For Bose this was a moment of deep pride and emotion. "I shall lead the army," he said, "when we march to India together." Yet in a sense, Bose seemed to be leaving them. Now they formed a part of the German army.

Fresh problems started. The German officers selected to command the Indian soldiers were not very good. They had no special love or feeling for the soldiers or the Indian cause.

As for the soldiers, their loyalty and discipline had to be constantly protected. They had changed loyalty once — from the British cause to the cause of Indian freedom. Now serving in a foreign land and owing loyality to a foreign power created its own problems.

Awaiting action in war, the soldiers also tended to become lazy. So it was decided to use them in some war or the other, before the actual attack on India. Bose insisted that these troops were only to be used

He Mentioned his wife only in a letter to his brother.

against British - Indian armies.

In January 1942, A.C.N. Nambiar, a communist journalist joined the Free India Centre. Bose gave him charge of a lot of work of the troops, and he became almost like a deputy leader. In fact after Bose left for the East, it was Nambiar who took charge of the Centre and its work.

A German lady named Fraulein Schenkl had been Bose's private secretary, ever since he started his work in Germany. She had also helped him earlier when he had written his book, 'The Indian Struggle' in 1934. Bose fell in love with her, and she was now secretly his wife. In September 1942, she gave birth to their daughter Anita.

Bose was under great stress because of his relationship with Fraulein Schenkl. He had once claimed that he would not marry till India was free. Now was also his reputation to consider. A marriage with a foreigner would start tongues wagging.

And so he kept it a secret. He mentioned his wife only in a letter to his brother, written just before he

Bose explained everything to Nambiar about his future plans.

left Germany for the Far East.

Bose had to wait for eight months before his journey to Japan could be arranged. No land route was open to him. It was the Japanese who helped, and they decided that the safest way to take Bose was by a submarine.

His Japanese friend, Colonel Yamamoto would have helped him with the arrangements; but he had already left for home through Turkey and Russia in November 1942.

While he waited, Bose explained everything to Nambiar about his future plans — opening new branches of the Free India Centre, broadcasting on radio, the studying of German police methods and the training of Indian seamen and airmen.

On January 26th 1943, he celebrated 'Independence Day' in Berlin with a great party. In order not to let people suspect his departure, he kept two recorded speeches for the radio to be broadcast after he left. In the speeches he also spoke about visits to the Russian front.

He and his men went abroad the ship 'Osorno' to follow Bose to Japan.

Bose had decided to take both his trusted assistants with him — Swami and another person called Abid Hassan, who had been with him ever since the training in Berlin began. But there was place for only one person, and so Hassan went with him.

The secret was so well kept that even Swami did not know. In March 1943, Swami received the transmitters which were being used by the Germans, and also the secret codes which would be used. Then on March 24, he and his men went aboard the ship 'Osorno' to follow Bose to Japan.

Even to those at the Free India Centre, the impression was that Bose had gone on a long tour.

Even though Nambiar took over the running of the Centre, in the absence of Bose, there was less interest and enthusiasm. In time, the Indians in Europe were swept without a struggle into the general confusion of Nazi break-up.

April 28th they were transferred by a rubber dinghy to the Japanese submarine.

XV

Subhash Chandra Bose and Abid Hassan left Kiel in a German U-Boat on February 8th, 1943. Past the Cape of Good Hope they went to a meting place 400 miles from the island of Madagascar.

Here on April 28th they were transferred by a rubber dinghy to the Japanese submarine I 29. It took them across the Indian Ocean to Sabang in Indonesia.

From here they flew to Tokyo with Colonel Yamamoto who was now the leader of the Japanese-India contact group, known as the Hikari Kikan. They reached Tokyo on June 13th, after a journey of 18 weeks.

Hassan was the only person with Bose on this long journey. He accepted the discomforts without protest; also the long silent hours of danger. He spent his time

He spent his time reading and making notes.

reading and making notes on his earlier book "The Indians Struggle'. He thought of the problems that awaited him in Japan.

Rash behari Basu had been a terrorist. He had already tried to talk to the Japanese about a treaty. But the Japanese replied, "You are not a Government, You are not a State, you have nothing to offer that we have not first given you; how then can you make treaties?"

Bose know that this was partly true and it had to be faced. But it had to be faced differently. They would have to form a temporary Indian Government with a strong Indian leadership.

Bose knew that under this government, he would have to collect as much money as possible. With a strong army worth the name, nobody could prevent him from taking over in the government of free India itself, in course of time.

Bose's achievements and reputation had reached the Far East well before him. His moving speeches, the contents of the book he had written so long ago

Soldiers and civilians gave Bose an enthusiastic welcome.

— had all made him famous. In fact his name was even used to gather together soldiers for the Indian National Army.

Soldiers and civilians gave Bose an enthusiastic welcome. His personal enthusiasm, his energy, his authority and his ideas of what was happening in the world, won him the real loyalty of Indians in East Asia. He swept people off their feet.

Bose was received by Tojo, the Japanese Prime Minister on the day after his arrival. Tojo made it clear that once the British were driven out of India, she would come under Japan. But this was only for military purpose — in case of another war. For all that, India would be independent in the true sense of the world.

For nearly two years Bose had waited for some such arrangement. He did not fear that the Japanese would rule India. They would have to do so with Japanese permission, especially if he had a strong Indian National Army. "Japan", said Bose, "is India's greatest friend."

On June 19th he held a press conference.

Bose was impressed by the Japanese. Their charm and sense of hard work on one hand and their barbaric savagery in war on the other.

Within a few days Rash Behari Basu informed him of all that was happening in the Indian National Army and the Japanese War Department. On June 19th he held a press conference, followed by two broadcasts on radio — once more he appealed to the people in India to extend their support to him and the work he was doing.

Indian freedom must be won with Indian blood. Only then would India understand how precious this freedom was — only then would she get the strength to preserve it.

Having strengthened his base abroad, Subhash Bose now appealed to India: "India shall be free and before long, a Free India will throw open the prison gates so that her worthy sons may step out of the darkness into the light of freedom, joy and self-fulfillment."

He reached Singapore on July 2nd.

XVI

Bose now decided that it was important to go to Singapore and reached there on July 2nd. He was given a tremendous welcome. There followed a week of public functions and private talks. Few people had met anyone like him — to each he seemed the answer to all problems they had faced so far.

On July 4th he accepted the Presidency of the "League" — the group formed Indians in South-East Asia. He stressed that all freedom fighters in India and outside must unite to strike a blow to the British Government in India.

"We have a grim fight ahead of us," he said, — "for the enemy is powerful and ruthless. In this final march to freedom you will have to face hunger, thirst, forced marches and death. Only when you pass this

Everywhere he went the audience cheered.

test, freedom will be yours."

On the next day he declared the existence of the Indian National Army to the world. This again was the proudest day of his life. "Let the battle cry be 'Chalo Delhi," he said.

This was followed by another parade at which the Japanese premier Tojo himself took the salute. Then on July 9th, 60,000 people stood to hear him in the pouring rain. He asked Indians in East Asia to volunteer themselves and their money for the war to be fought.

Everywhere he went his audience cheered — they adored him, they pledged their support and devotion to him. In August he attended the Burmese Independence celebrations in Rangoon.

He visited Bangkok and Saigon. There were more speeches, interviews and long meeting with Japanese commanders and officials. He worked tirelessly far into the night and slept little.

When he heard of the famine in Bengal in the summer of 1943, he offered 100,000 tons of rice to be shipped to India as a gift from the League. The

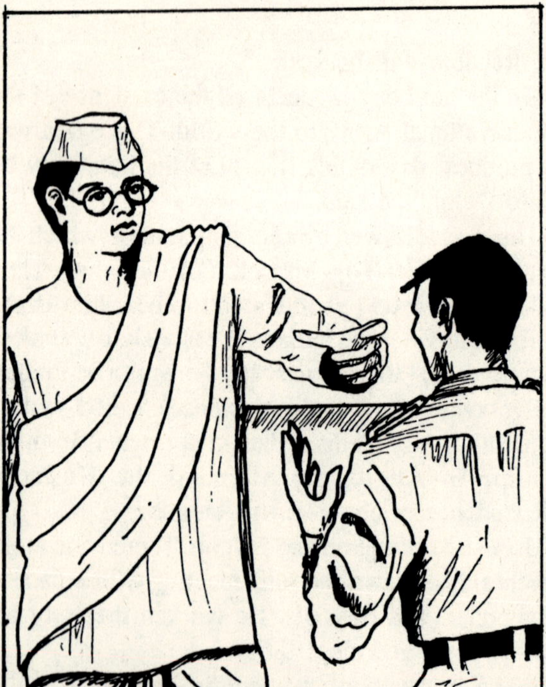

"Any freedom of India got by Japanese sacrifices," he said, "is worse than slavery!"

offer was ignored, and he attacked the government and the new Viceroy Lord Wavell for being indifferent to the plight of Indians. On August 25th he took over command of the INA. With Field Marshall Count Terauchi, the commander of the Japanese army in South-East Asia, he spoke about the INA joining the effort in their attack on Imphal. But Terauchi was not very keen, and said,

"These soldiers have just been defeated in Malaya and further, they are not as tough as the Japanese fighters; and what is there to prevent them from going across to their friends in India once we reach?"

But Bose had different ideas. He did not want Japan to free India. He wanted as many India soldiers there as possible. Only then would the victory mean anything for Indians.

"Any freedom for India got by Japanese sacrifices," he said, "is worse than salvery!"

Terauchi at last agreed to use the regiment as a trial. If this was equal to the Japanese standards, then rest of the army would be sent for.

He set a personal example to his troops

Bose started planning after hearing this promise. The Ist INA Division was re-formed and sent to North Malaya for training. Next he went about the major task of motivating his soldiers — unless they were mentally

strong and energetic, they could never win against an enemy that was powerful, better equipped and more in number.

For this he set about building up the confidence of his leaders and the spirit of the soldiers. Bose knew that the present state of the INA was bad — it was lazy and ill-disciplined. Desertions were common and there was even disloyal talk.

Bose spoke openly — all this would have to stop. Those who had the strength to change should stay; the rest were free to leave. For those who remained with him, he would do his best — pensions for the families of those who had died fighting, care of the wounded and rewards for the brave.

He set a personal example to his troops—his smart uniform, the heroic pose, the expression on his face

Women also played their part in the Rani of Jhansi Regiment.

of strong determination. He treated his troops as his equals, and his door was always open to them.

During September the chosen men of the Ist Division came together as the 'Subhash Regiment' under Captain Shah Nawaz, one of the best officers under Bose. The regiment underwent hard training until it began its to move to Burma on November 20th.

The other regiments were soon filled up with new recruits from training centres in Malaya, Siam, Burma and South China. Women also played their part as nurses and soldiers in the Rani of Jhansi Regiment founded.

The group left by submarine.

XVII

Bose knew that something had to be done about sending good spies to India for gaining information. So far out of the 130 Indians sent to India none had returned.

Swami, who had come with Bose from Germany organised the new group with the help of some German equipment which he had got with him.

In October, Bose himself spoke to his group of people about whom to meet in India. Their job was to collect military information. These agents were to report by wireless from Punjab, Bombay and Bengal. They would have to contact revolutionary group in India.

Bose warned his agents to take risks only when necessary. Finally the group left by submarine on

It was nearly 6 am. by the time he completed it.

December 8th and disembarked on the Kathiawar coast between Bombay and Karachi, fourteen days later. This group was in India with its wireless sets for less than two months.

Bose inaugurated the "Provisional Government" (or temporary government) of India on October 21st. Bose had to fight many battles with the Japanese with regards to this. Bose wrote out his Proclamation and formed his Cabinet.

He declared himself as 'Head of State, Prime Minister and Minister for war and foreign Affairs'. At first he appointed only four other ministers, eight military representatives, and eight civilian advisers.

Bose himself wrote out the Proclamation—starting before dawn on October 20th, writing swiftly in pencil, sheet after sheet. There was never a backward glance or correction.

It was nearly 6 am. by the time he completed it, sipping black coffee since midnight.

At a grand ceremony Bose and his Cabinet took the oath:

October 23rd, the provisional Government declared war on Britain and the USA.

"In the name of God, I take this sacred oath that to liberate India and the thirty eight crores of my countrymen, I will continue the sacred war of freedom till the last breath of my life..."

The National Anthem was a poem of Rabindranath Tagore, which had also been sung in Germany — now it was translated into Hindustani and set to music by a soldier. As it was sung everyone present stood up; there were cheers and slogans. It almost seemed as if the day of freedom had come.

At midnight on October 23rd, the Provisional Government declared war on Britain and the USA. Not all in the cabinet wanted to include USA, but Bose was firm.

Recognition of this government came after some weeks — from Japan, Burma, Germany, Phillipines, Nanking and Siam.

Now as always, money was the single greatest problem. Bose was drawn in two directions. He knew that the INA had to depend on Japan for money. But this did not mean that they had to work according

In April 1943, the Japanese attack on Imphal was planned.

to Japanese commands.

When Bose asked for donations, at first money came in quite fast. But this did not last. And Bose even had to make threats to the rich Indians — "We have to achieve independence by any means," he said," and if you think your wealth and property are your own you are wrong... your lives and money now belong to India and India alone."

The 2nd INA Division was formed in December 1943. But all was not well at the training centres. In November there had been a serious mutiny — some of the soldiers had revolted because of the hard discipline and discomfort.

Desertions in the INA were common, and this was soon declared as a crime to be punished by death.

In April 1943, the Japanese attack on Imphal was planned. The object of this attack was to stop British from invading Burma in 1944, and set up Japanese defence on the frontier mountains.

The plot was to first defeat the British in the mountain region of the Arakean. Then during April,

Kohima and Imphal could be captured slowly without danger of their being re-armed with British troops.

With the starting of monsoon by the end of May, everything would come to a halt. The Japanese thought that the British would get no time to prepare fresh defence east of the River Brahmaputra. So that when the rains stopped the whole of Assam and East Bengal would lie open to the Japanese.

Such was the ambitious plan. What happened was perhaps the worst military tragedy for INA who had joined forces with the Japanese.

XVIII

"The first drop of blood to be shed on Indian soil should be that of a member of the INA," declared Bose. He insisted that all three battalions of the Subhash Regiment be used independently in the attack.

The Japanese Commander-in-Chief General Kawabe offered two roles for the Suhbash Regiment — the first battalion was to form part of the group attacking the British in the Kalasan Valley, while the other two were to help a Japanese battalion to guard the roads over the China Hills.

Bose spent much of his time talking to the officers, encouraging the men building up their fighting spirit. On February 3rd he bade them farewell. As Netaji watched the trains move away, he had tears in his eyes.

On April 7th, 1944, the Imphal attack was in full swing.

The Japanese army had not taken very kindly to the INA. They felt that the INA was made up of defeated soldiers, who had switched loyalties. They could never be trusted even though there was great respect for Bose. Knowing this, Bose fought for his men at every step.

It was months before Bose knew that the Arakan battle had ended in shattering defeat for the Japanese.

Bose was busy trying to organise the group of men who would have to take care of those Indian territories which were captured by the Japanese. General Mutaguchi in Maymyo sent a specific message to Bose about this.

Even though Bose never worried about the intentions of the Japanese in India, the plan was clear: the Japanese meant to control India in the same way as they already controlled Burma.

On April 7th, 1944, with the Imphal attack in full swing, Japan took up a small headquarters to the little hilltown of Maymyo near Mandalay. Bose waited to hear about the fall of Imphal so that his life's ambition

Bose had received reports from the battlefield.

of finally freeing India could begin.

General Mutaguchi who was in charge of the Imphal attack was still in Maymyo. He was not worried about the great distance that now separated the commander from his troops, and if the Japanese had given permission, he would have gone to his men.

On April 25th Mutaguchi admitted that there was a problem. By now Bose also had received reports from the battlefield. Colonel M.Ź. Kiani of the INA wrote from his headquarters, some 35 miles from Imphal, pleading that he needed the help of the rest of the Subhash Regiment.

Shah Nawaz from the Chin Hills told of the hardships his men were suffering. The Ground was difficult, rations were poor, there was much malaria and no medicines.

It was many months before Bose had any realisation of the disaster. He tried to do all he could to attend to the problems faced by the men battlefield. But accurate reports did not reach him till the end of June.

He returned to Rangoon so that he could get news

The Japanese had given him an eleven-seater aircraft called 'Azad Hind'.

faster and also fly quickly to Imphal if required — the Japanese had just given him an eleven - seater aircraft called 'Azad Hind'.

He still continued to address meetings and collect funds. And there was the job of looking into the affairs of the training centres as well. For example, there was the sad case of the death of a Tamil recruit.

The evidence was clear — the Commanding Officer had been high-handed and cruel. He was dismissed as soon as the enquiry was completed.

Disloyalty was another thing that Bose could never tolerate. One of the officers, Captain Durrani was suspected of sending men to India in order to surrender and pass information about the INA to those in India.

Bose was very angry. When Durrani was tortured to confess, Bose did not stop the Japanese. And even after, undergoing worst torture, Durrani refused to admit anything.

For this act of withstanding torture, Durrani was awarded the George Cross in 1946. Even though Bose did not order the torture, he could not escape

The Allied forces led by Britain attacked Europe.

responsibility for what happened.

Meanwhile, the Allied forces led by Britain attacked Europe; America won many successes in the Pacific. But Bose still remained confident of Japanese success — because for him, the freedom was linked to it.

Rations, transport and ammunition-were totally lacking.

XIX

The decision to withdraw from Imphal was announced on July 26th. August saw the full horror of disaster. The trouble had been that when the Japanese had called the 1st Division of the INA to the front they had already failed in their plan.

They had hoped to capture Indian positions by this time. Food and clothing for the INA which was to be given by the Japanese was impossible — the Japanese did not have enough even for themselves. So rations, transport and ammunition — all essential things — were totally lacking.

Very often the Japanese took away things which Bose had tried to provide for INA. But nothing, Bose and his assistants could do at this late stage would have helped.

The Indian Army met pitiful, starving and totally demoralised INA soldiers, crawling up to them.

The Indian Army which followed the retreating Japanese met pitiful, starving and totally demoralised INA soldiers, crawling up to them, pointing out others of their comrades, too weak to move. With the hundreds of bodies of Japanese dead, were found many of the INA who had died of starvation.

All this was reported in August that made Bose realise the full extent of the disaster that had struck his troops. He was shocked. He threw his full energy trying to do what he could for the wounded.

On August 19th, Colonel Kiani, sent a pathetic appeal — to save hundreds of sick men who were struck by floods on the withdrawal route. Bose was helpless — even the Japanese in Rangoon were out of touch with the situation and could do nothing.

Even though Bose was terribly angry with the fate of the INA in battle, he did not say anything in public. He still spoke of British defeat. In private he pulled up the officers who had been in action and blamed them for the defeat. But it was not just the officers who had brought on failure.

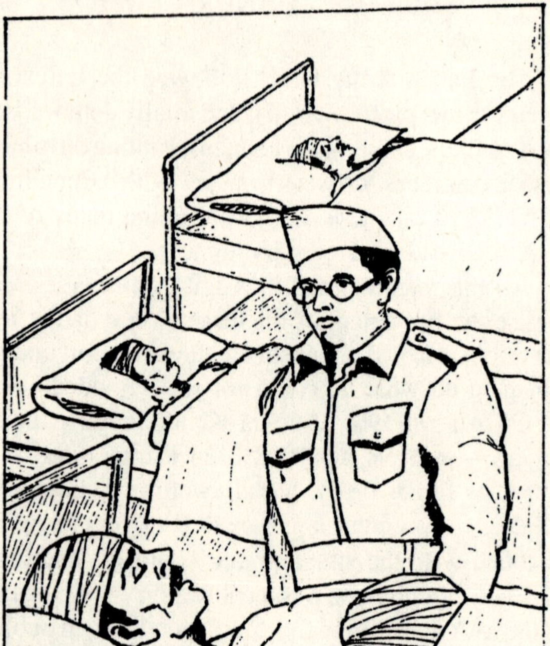

His visits now helped.

Bose even felt that it was a personal defeat. Of the six thousand men he had sent to Imphal, fifteen hundred had deserted or been captured. Only ten thousand six hundred returned.

On September 18th he left for North Burma and saw things for himself. Everywhere he saw suffering and heard pitiful tales of defeat and retreat. But his visits now helped — for he was able to inspire much devotion, love and passionate sincerity to his work.

Bose felt that he had failed to turn his men into heroes. He had even failed to instigate the loyalty in the Indian Army. Bose also realised that the next time he would have to be in direct command of the INA, without the Japanese interference.

For this he started making agreements with the Japanese. Even at this stage, since he was aware of what was happening in the world, he knew that Japan was doomed. He hoped that they would last just long enough for a new attack on India from Burma.

Air attacks on Japan and South-East Asia had increased. The INA was asked to keep its troops in

Air attacks on Japan and South-East Asia had increased.

Malaya for defence against British attacks. The number of recruits wanting to join the INA had reduced.

Bose made one more attempt to improve things. He spoke to senior INA officers, toured the country, asked for money contributions and punished those who did not listen.

In December 1944, the Japanese were defeated by the single division of the British Army positioned at the Mayn Valley in the Arakan Hills. The Japanese had hoped to recover these positions which they had lost in the last battle.

The British advanced further, gathering up the INA as they went on without stopping. By the end of January out of the 160 of the INA soldiers, only 40 found their way back across the hills of Rangoon.

On January 14th, the Japanese were driven back further. Bose had reached Burma on January 12th, eager to take part in the new victories which the Japanese were still planning. Major Dhillon with the 4th Gureilla Regiment was ordered to hold the 12 miles south of Nyaungu, down the Irrawaddy River.

The 2nd INA Infantry Battalion was rushed here and ordered to patrol the Western slopes of Mount Popa.

The Japanese did not know that the British force planning this attack was huge in number. Major Dhillon's Regiment numbered barely 1200.

Before the INA could dig its treches, the British had crossed over---unsuccessful at first and then helped by the large number of deserters from the INA, who had surrendered before even putting up a fight.

The British soon occupied Nyaungu and Pagan, and Dhillon withdrew his remaining troops 35 miles to the south-east on the road to Meiktila. Japanese troops were rushed to bar the way to Meiktila.

The 2nd INA Infantry Battalion was also rushed here and ordered to patrol to the west and north on the Western slopes of Mount Popa, a steep isolated 5000 foot mountain.

At this point on February 18th, Bose left Rangoon to tour the front. He hoped that his presence would boost the spirits of his troops.

Shah Nawaz and others delayed his departure.

XX

At Meiktila all was confusion with the Japanese trying to desperately do something under heavy air attacks. Bose heard with a shock about the desertions at Nyaungu. He ordered that if any deserters were found, they were to be arrested or shot dead.

Shah Nawaz visited Sahgal, who was commanding the regiment at Popa, and found that Dhillon had been given an impossible task. He reported this to Bose in Meiktila on February 25th.

Bose wanted to rush to Mount Popa to die fighting with his men. Shah Nawaz and others delayed his departure. "Your life is not your own," they said, "it is a precious trust for India; we are responsible..."

On February 25th one British column was stationed barely 16 miles away. Bose did not wish to be trapped

For days, sick with shock, he kept to his room.

along with the Japanese at Meiktila; and so decided to get away with Shah Nawaz.

As they left they wondered if they were being followed. On March 2nd an urgent message came from headquarters in Rangoon. There the most shattering news awaited him. Five staff officers at Mount Popa had deserted: Further desertions seemed certain.

Bose was stunned: for days, sick with shock, he kept to his room. This was his only real moment of defeat and he faced it alone.

He came out of the depression, calm and withdrawn.

At the end of April, everything was finished. May 13th Shah Nawaz, Dhillon about fifty men surrendered — the story of the 2nd INA division was over.

The Japanese hurried to move out of Rangoon, as the British Division moved in.

During this time Bose was busy with matters of the INA. He would often feel like withdrawing and just laying down his life. But he knew that his work was still incomplete.

"Go down as heroes."

The women in the Rani of Jhansi Regiment had to be sent home safely to their parents. He also tried to move the three thousand unfit men in Rangoon to a safer place in Siam. For the future, he had decided that as long as the Japanese were willing to hold out in Rangoon, he would fight to the end.

The large INA camps outside the city, which contained six thousand soldiers, were organised to help in the last battle. But even some of these had to withdraw when the Japanese retreat from Rangoon became final on April 23rd.

Bose left with a few ministers and senior officers and the last group of women on the night of April 24th.

Major General Loganadhan was left to take charge of the INA surrender in Rangoon. In his last message as he left Rangoon Bose said, "I do not leave Burma of my own free will. I would have liked to stay and share with you the sorrow of temporary defeat."... "Go down as heroes," he said, "go down upholding the highest code of honour and discipline."

Seven hundred and fifty of the ex-Indian Army officers and men were shipped to India for investigations.

On May 4th, the British entered Rangoon and took charge. Seven hundred and fifty of the ex-Indian Army officers and men were shipped to India for investigations. In the months that followed, many thousands had to be sent from Rangoon, and then from Malaya and Bangkok.

Bose had covered the last ten miles to the Sitang River on foot.

EPILOGUE

In his weary march from Rangoon to Siam, Bose felt that perhaps he should seek refuge in Russia. He felt utterly downcast and beaten with the shattering of his dream. But his mind remained on the purpose at hand.

Bose had covered the last ten miles to the Sitang River on foot. At last the Japanese found lorries to carry his men—and till then, Bose continued to march with his men, determined to share in their suffering and hardship.

He reached the Siamesse capital on May 15th, and tried to get together his cabinet. There was still a hope that Japan would recover from the defeat in Burma. But if it lost in the final run, Russia was the only place for him.

From Bangkok Bose continued to make speeches

Bose realised that the basic enemity of Russia towards the west would help in gaining her friendship; he also realised that Russia was moving towards becoming a powerful country.

From Bangkok, Bose continued to make speeches calling on the Indians of South-East Asia to increase their efforts. "We may not travel to Delhi," he said, "via Imphal' but we shall get there all right."

At this point the Viceroy of India, Lord Wavell, announced new proposals for settling the situation in India. Bose flew to Singapore on June 18th to speak on Singapore radio — the Bangkok Radio was no longer working.

Bose did not believe that a solution could be found on peaceful terms — he did not trust the British, he did not trust the Congress leadership and he did not understand the need to give in to forming the separate State of Pakistan.

But his voice was the only discordant note in all the plans that were being finalised between the Indian leaders and the British. There was no doubt now in

At about 2 am. on August 13th, two of his advisers arrived from Singapore.

the country, that the British meant to hand over power to the Indians — they were trying to see how best they could do it in the shortest possible time.

Bose meanwhile continued with his efforts in Malaysia and Singapore — collecting funds, negotiating with the Japanese, trying to convince the people there and in India of the grave mistakes the Congress had committed.

In the early hours of August 11th when Bose was investigating the case of a mutiny at the INA training camp at Seremban, he learned that Russia had declared war on Japan. He did not let this disturb his work.

Next day he received a message asking him to come back to Singapore. He wondered how far the Russians had moved and what position Japan would now take.

At about 2 am. on August 13th, two of his advisers arrived from Singapore to tell him that Japan was about to surrender. He said, "So that is it. Now, what next?"

Bose reached Singapore on the evening of August 13. He had to tie up details on the using of INA funds

Finally Bose left for Bangkok with Lieutenant Colonel Habib-ur-Rehman.

and other routine matters. The INA would have to surrender as well and the Records would have to be destroyed.

Bose himself was undecided — should he stay on and surrender as he wanted to, or should he get away, make a fresh start elsewhere and continue his efforts for an armed struggle in India against the British?

Once again he was forced to leave by his ministers and advisers. Whom should he take with him? He wanted to take as many of his ministers and chief advisers as possible, but all would not come. Most of them were not even there with him when he took the decision of leaving.

Finally Bose left for Bangkok with Lieutenant-Colonel Habib-ur-Rehman, the INA Chief-of Staff, to confer with senior Japanese leaders. From here, the group that left for Saigon on August 17th consisted of General Isoda, General Hachiya, Abid Hassan and two other advisers.

At Saigon General Isoda offered one seat in an aircraft bound for Tokyo via Dairen in Manchuria.

The Plane, a twin-engine bomber took off at 5.15 pm.

Bose wondered if he should go alone. He must not seem to be running away, but there was no sense in being captured either.

At last the Japanese agreed to allow one more passenger and Habib-ur-Rehman went with Bose — the rest of the party would follow.

It was a hurried, confused parting. "Jai Hind," he said, as he shook hands with those he was leaving, 'I will see you later."

The plane, a twin-engine bomber took off at 5.15 pm., and landed at Tourane in French Indo-China later the same evening. Next day the flight took off again and reached Taihoku in Formosa at about 2 pm. on August 18th.

The passengers had lunch while the plane refuelled. At about 2.30 pm., just after it had taken off again, the plane caught fire, dived steeply and crashed. With the other survivors, Bose and Habib-ur-Reshman struggled from the wreckage.

Bose's clothes were on fire and he had head injuries besides the terrible burns on his face and body. Even

The plane caught fire, dived steeply and crashed.

before he reached hospital he knew that he would not recover.

Habib-ur-Rehman was at his bedside throughout the day. It was clear that nothing could save him. A few minutes before the end, he spoke to his companion: "Habib," he said, "I feel that I shall die very soon. I have fought for India's freedom until the last. Tell my countrymen 'India will be free before long'; Long live free India.'

Shortly afterwards he breathed his last. The death of Subhash Chandra Bose shrouds in mystery. There are a handful of his audent followers, who believe that he did not die in that fateful crash.

News of the crash did not reach the outside would till August 21st, 1945. Everywhere Indians mourned for this brave hero, who spurning personal gains, had lived for the motherland. There always remained an undying hope in the hearts of millions, that Subhash Chandra would appear again when the time was right.

JAICO PUBLISHING HOUSE

Elevate Your Life. Transform Your World.

ESTABLISHED IN 1946, Jaico Publishing House is home to world-transforming authors such as Sri Sri Paramahansa Yogananda, Osho, the Dalai Lama, Sri Sri Ravi Shankar, Sadhguru, Robin Sharma, Deepak Chopra, Jack Canfield, Eknath Easwaran, Devdutt Pattanaik, Khushwant Singh, John Maxwell, Brian Tracy, and Stephen Hawking.

Our late founder Mr. Jaman Shah first established Jaico as a book distribution company. Sensing that independence was around the corner, he aptly named his company Jaico ('Jai' means victory in Hindi). In order to service the significant demand for affordable books in a developing nation, Mr. Shah initiated Jaico's own publications. Jaico was India's first publisher of paperback books in the English language.

While self-help, religion and philosophy, mind/body/spirit, and business titles form the cornerstone of our non-fiction list, we publish an exciting range of travel, current affairs, biography, and popular science books as well. Our renewed focus on popular fiction is evident in our new titles by a host of fresh young talent from India and abroad. Jaico's recently established translations division translates selected English content into nine regional languages.

Jaico distributes its own titles. With its headquarters in Mumbai, Jaico has branches in Ahmedabad, Bangalore, Chennai, Delhi, Hyderabad, and Kolkata.

SINCE